TIME WILL TELL

TIME WILL TELL

COURTNEY PEPPERNELL

Andrews McMeel
PUBLISHING®

Acknowledgments

I wanted to start by thanking my team—James, Katherine, Karna, Justin, Byron, and all those at Andrews McMeel Universal, especially Patty, Liz, and Diane—for their effort in helping to create this book. The support and production efforts never go unnoticed, and it would not be possible without each of you. Thank you to my family, as always, for your unwavering support through endless days and nights of my creative process. These books have become such an integral part of my life and my career, and it is through my support network that I am able to do what I love to do.

And finally thank you, of course, to my readers. I say this often, but I say it because it is true. You have given me a platform, and there are many days I cannot fathom why, but nevertheless I do not take the responsibility lightly. I am so glad you are continuing this journey with me.

All my love!

This book contains strong themes; read with care.

Instagram: @courtneypeppernell
TikTok: @courtneypeppernell
Twitter: @CourtPeppernell
Email: courtney@pepperbooks.org
www.peppernell.com

If you look beyond the horizon, far past the light and all the things burning bright, you will find an ancient kingdom, filled with rolling clouds, and sun showers, and all the earth's wondrous wisdom. Within this kingdom live guides as far as the eye can see, and they hold a most important role, of bringing us back to whom we know ourselves to be.

One day, a soul fell from the stars, crashing through mountains and rough seas; it landed in the deepest part of a familiar forest, filled with tall evergreen trees. The soul had been lost, long ago, a broken thing that the world had forgotten, a fragile heart, invisible and no longer seen.

This particular day, the struggle of the soul was unbearable, a weight that forced all light into the shadows. An endless darkness ensued, one that felt singular, as though nobody else understood and nobody else cared to know.

This soul was you, and this is the story of many things— of reflection and repair, of change and rebirth, of knowing that the greatest fight we face is our will to cling to this life on Earth.

Out of the shadows, a guide appeared, with soft silk robes and a floral crown and eyes brighter than the sun. The guide said, "There you are. I've been looking for you, our little lost one."

"I am broken," you replied through tears, "reduced to nothing more than ash and dust." The guide looked back at you sincerely and said, "But it is in these moments we must look within and fight with all we have, to regain our trust."

The guide reached for you gently and wrapped you tightly in a cocoon, hung you from the nearest branch, far from harm's reach, and whispered, "Believe me now; there are so many things that life can teach."

"How," you asked, "can I choose to go on, when life is so hard and the world is a little strange?"

And the guide smiled, soft and true, "Because I am here, and I will be here through your journey of change."

So, within the cocoon, this safe space, you found a place to retreat and heal. To understand that all the ache is a just another chance to feel. You began to reflect on your loss, learning that to start is to acknowledge the things deep within your heart. To survive is to open yourself up to repair, to understand that not all things in life are fair, but this does not diminish your worth, your spark, or your flair.

And through all the learning and all the changing, you learned one of life's greatest lessons, one that can take some time to know to be true—you will always awaken as someone bolder, someone brighter, and someone new.

But perhaps, most importantly, this is the story of how you emerged more beautiful and stronger than the moment you fell.

And as it happens, like all things in life, time will tell.

How to Care for a Cocoon

You will need

Through . . .

. . . time will tell

The Reflecting

Time Will Tell

My life collapsed
the moment my heart
stopped beating.

Its rhythm connected
to all the things
I loved and all the joy
I found in every day.

Suddenly, I had no joy,
no will, no purpose.
And so, my heart, it stopped.

It stopped seeing the beauty
in all the things around me,
it stopped listening to reason,
it stopped feeling the sun
as it shone so beautifully
in the morning.

And it was during this time
I retreated—

I decided that in order to
come to terms with losing
my heart, my mind, my soul,
I needed somewhere warm,
somewhere the thoughts could
just be thoughts.

So, I wrapped myself
tightly in a silk cocoon.

And I told myself that
the only way I was going
to survive was if I slowed
down my healing and I *gently*
reasoned with all my being.

Because to reason with yourself
is to reflect, and to reflect must
always start with rest.

It felt like the world stood still,
the day we said our goodbyes.
And the earth split open, like a
heart cracking right down the middle.
And what poured from this open
void were all the feelings left
unresolved and words unsaid.

We should have spoken these things
out into the open, rather than allow
them to stay in the shadows, where
they only grew darker and angrier.
We should have released the way we
felt, instead of letting the silence fill
every space that ever surrounded us.

All those seconds, minutes, and hours
I wanted to say *I love you, I'm sorry,*
let's talk, let's just try again.
Instead, I allowed too much pride inside,
and it forced me to look the other way.

And I can't undo any of it—not now.
If I could do it all again, I would have
been braver, wiser, more willing to
run in the same direction you were running.
But our paths no longer run together.

I should have told you
I should have told you
I should have told you

It took time to live with the loss of you.

One minute you were a living, breathing, beautiful thing, and the next you were gone. The world lost light, and I lost the love of my life.

And the loss kept repeating.

Every time I heard your favorite song or found a missing item of clothing. Every movie I watched alone and walk I took with only my own feet hitting the pavement. We were in sync once upon a time, and now the rhythm is different. So too the way people look at me, as though I won't make it through the night.

But I will.

I will rise, because in those deepest moments of loss, it is your hand I feel, pulling me back above the water.

Time Will Tell

A room is just a room
if not filled with the
things that make us smile
and laugh and beam with pride.

A day is just a day
if not made up of moments
that make us feel alive
and convince us not to hide.

A year is just a year
if not spent with those we love
to remind us we can do more
than just survive.

A life is just a life
if not reflected upon often
and memories fondly
thought of
from time to time.

You have lost someone, and the wound is so fresh; you are caught between wanting to fill it with daisies and joy or stitching it back together and never speaking of what caused the pain in the first place.

But this person was important to you—so important that you wrapped pieces of yourself around them, entwined, tangled, like a heart for a heart and a soul for a soul. Now that they are gone, you cannot seem to remember what the pieces looked like or felt like before they became so tangled.

But tomorrow, you will awake once more and feel just a little lighter. And the next day, you will awake again and feel lighter still. Until weeks will go by, and months too, and the loss will feel small—not insignificant, because the loss will always matter, but it will be but only one piece, instead of the entire puzzle that is you.

Just one small piece.

This life has given me many beautiful things, many opportunities to smile. Many moments to stop and admire, stare up at the stars for a while. But it has also given me shadows, and doubts, and losses that have felt so all-consuming there was no longer any joy to dream about. But of all the times I have sat with such loss, such grief, I have found the most beautiful thing a person can do is to listen. Let me speak of such devastating things into the wind, so that they may be carried off with the dandelions. Let me cry, rage, despair over the things that have ripped me apart, so that, in time, they no longer sit and well in my heart.

FORGET-ME-NOT

One springtime, I rented an old boathouse by the lake. I thought perhaps the sun rising over the water each morning would remind me of being alive, of what it means to find hope when I felt so lost.

During my second week at the lake, I stumbled across an old walking track, lined with maple trees. The red and orange leaves filled so much space, every time I ventured farther along the path, I thought I might just disappear.

But I continued along the path, finding more and more maple trees. Until, farther to the end, where the mountain met the lake, I stumbled upon a tiny little house with blue shutter windows and a golden door.

It is here I met a woman who grew forget-me-not flowers in her garden. Each day, I returned to the woman and watched as she delicately tended to her flowers.

And one day she turned to me and said, "Do you know what happens when you lose yourself? You stare at the same spot in the sky for hours, hoping to find a smile hidden in the clouds, anything to remind you that you are still alive in the world. You think about moments in your life, but they're often in pieces, as though you have forgotten your place in your own memories. You eat little, forget to shower, wonder if this version of yourself will ever shed, like peeling back a layer of dying skin."

The woman pointed at me and said, "You have lost yourself."

And with a sad heart, I asked her, "What do I do?"

The woman turned from me, went deep into the rows of flowers, and returned moments later, to hand me a forget-me-not.

"They are the memory flower," she said. "They tell stories, share memories, talk of the beautiful things in life. Sometimes, late in the afternoon, when the light of the day touches the tips of their petals, I can hear them whispering."

I stared down at the flower in my hands, delicate, soft, all but an earthly memory.

"Do you think we can be found, even when we are lost?"

And she just smiled. "To find is to remember."

SHORELINE HEART

My heart was the infinite open shoreline
and you the constant wave, always
colliding, crashing, and breaking
washing away memories and dreams

and the sun would rise each morning
so beautiful in all its wondrous light
and it was in this golden light that I
would search for answers—

aching to keep you longer than the day before
wanting to hold on to you forever
but as the day faded, so too would you
sliding away, back to the deep ocean

and so, I, left on the shore, hand over heart
would stare up at the moon and stars
wishing she would wash you back again
tides changing, heart breaking, always

hoping

The loss had settled itself into my heart
the same way the stars had settled
into the velvet night—
hanging, burning, infinite

It became a pillar holding me at bay
but after awhile, it began to crack
unable to withstand the weight
of the heartache I was forced to carry

my heart a broken home, with no light
every mirror reflected only the sadness
every window barred shut to the world
every doorway sealed as day is to the night

the loss was everywhere.

Time Will Tell

You will wage a war
between self-love
and self-destruction
more than once in your life.

But often when buildings
burn down and turn to ash
people come from miles to rebuild.

The way back home
isn't always to be
walked alone.

You will meet souls
along the way
who will offer guidance
and reassurance.

You will meet souls
who will offer a hand.
Don't be afraid to reach
out to others
in order to pull yourself
back up again.

The doubt will always
find you in the unexpected
moments, sometimes even
on a day that is going fine.

But the doubt is never
the enemy, just a reminder,
to continue to push forward,
with every breath
and every moment in time.

The sadness was someone knocking at my door, but I could not hear them. Instead, I was buried in pillows that felt as though they may swallow me whole. It was reading my favorite book, unable to understand the words. It was listening to my favorite song, unable to truly hear the music. It was staring up at the ceiling, hoping it may fall down on top of me and end all this misery.

And yet, the knocking persisted. Each and every day, the knocking continued. Until, finally, I opened the door, and you were standing on the other side. With arms filled with new books and new pillows.

You folded yourself around me and whispered that today was a new day. That even in the moments I could not bring myself to get up off the floor, there would always be someone knocking at my door.

A broken heart
isn't always measured
by the ache
that follows
with every old photo
or memory

It is the fear you hold
that you will never fall
in love again

The fear of having
to learn someone new
and not knowing
if they want to learn
you too.

They don't teach you that you will always be searching and learning. Even long after the textbooks have grown dust and the exams have finished, you will still continue discovering. It is in these experiences, this journey through every new month and every new year, that you find your ability to never stop this learning.

You come to understand that not all things will be in your control. Not all things in life can be explained in a textbook or measured in how many words you wrote in that final essay.

And the most important, perhaps, is understanding that even on the days the tears fall and your body aches, it does not mean your existence was ever a mistake.

Then suddenly it was over.
We were no longer the people
we promised we would be
to each other.

I left many notes behind,
hoping you might stumble
across them one day,
hold them fondly.

Be reminded of our love,
not as ending but of a beautiful
and unwavering memory.

But, of course, I knew someone
else would move into your heart
someday.

And I have always wondered
if she would write you notes
in the same way I did.

I've been spending my time
relearning my heart.

I've been taking steps to enjoy
the silence rather than see it
as the enemy.

To find refuge in reflecting.

I've been reminding myself
that no one is really ready
until they're ready.

But the trouble with shouldering
all the world's heartache and all the suffering
is that you begin to feel responsible.

You convince your heart that
it must carry these burdens
as though they have been stitched
into your entire being all along
all day (day), all night (night) long.

After awhile, your seams start to fray
bursting with the weight of the world
your aching shoulders becoming torn
ripped inch by inch and stitch by stitch
for all the world's suffering is far too
much for just one person to carry alone.

It is not your responsibility to shoulder
the worries and burdens of others.
It is not your responsibility to climb
every mountain or sail every sea.

But it is your responsibility to breathe
and to always be all that you can be.

But it can be difficult to talk about how you are feeling when you don't always understand it yourself. How can you explain these thoughts running through your mind when you don't truly know why they are there in the first place? But even if your heart feels lost and your mind cluttered, know that despite every thought working against you, these thoughts will always be important. They will always be part of the journey. These thoughts of defeat are not here to ruin you; they are here to remind you of how much you matter.

We are taught to hold on tighter
to the things we do not wish
to let go of—like a balloon, or
a hat in the wind, or a pair of
sunglasses while on a boat
traveling steadfast up the river

Hold on, we are told, *do not let go*

And so too I held on tighter to you
for the longer I held on, then perhaps
the more we would learn to grow

But neither of us really did grow
We became stuck, barely able
to find our own light in all the
darkness we brought upon the other

When we finally pulled apart
I knew how sad you were; I was
sad too; I loved you more than
all the things I thought I knew

But by finally choosing to let you go
I was able to slowly start to grow—
no longer empty, no longer hollow

There will come a time when you are not searching for the answers at the bottom of a bottle. A time when getting out of bed and starting your day doesn't feel like the worst thing in the world. Your heart won't look for love in all the wrong places; the days won't feel like all these empty spaces. Someone will come into your life and not judge you for the choices you have made. They will listen to you, support you, remind you that you are just as special too.

There I was, and all I could hear were the thoughts in my heart, fracturing my very soul, completely falling apart.

Too afraid to dance on my own, too afraid to fall asleep in the dark, too afraid to let myself feel, too afraid of the next moment around the bend, because I was drowning in the deep end.

I know you could see the way everything was spiraling out of control, and I was just so desperate to find my way back home.

I need you to lift me back up, tell me everything is going to find its way again—the flowers will regrow, the sun will shine once more, I won't always be drowning in so many dark thoughts, your love will be mine again.

Time Will Tell

For the longest time, she wanted it all to end.
She dreamt of leaving, of throwing herself
to the stars and saying goodbye to the world.

But through the thoughts and the darkest parts
of her mind, she came to realize that it was not
the leaving she wanted most but for relief from
the darkness—for the shadow to become a friend.

Because if she showed a little patience and a little
kindness to the things that made her ache, in return,
she would notice the color in the sky and the
symphony of the rain.

She would come to know that in her life,
despite all its chaos, she could triumph over the pain.

In the middle of the beating rhythm of everyday life, and the habit of living, she would unpack her grief from the space in her heart in which it lived.

And she would let the grief sit with her a moment while she remembered what it felt like when it took up the most space in her heart.

How it felt like the sun swallowing the horizon, like a song she did not know the words to, like a map with faded lines going nowhere, and a tree in winter left bare. Oh, how heavy it felt, as though she would never again have room for anything else.

She hadn't been sure she would survive, if she would outlive all the ache and pain. Yet she did survive, and she learned that loss was what it meant to be human—you begin again and again.

A CONVERSATION WITH LOSS

There were many days and nights before Loss and I met. First, I housed Denial and then Anger and then Despair. But after many months of hiding, Loss finally showed up on my door, and as I stepped aside and allowed it into my home, Loss had looked at me and told it was time to stop.

So, I did. I stopped reading, writing, and watering the plants. I stopped going for walks in my favorite lavender fields; I stopped searching for the tallest sunflower to whisper words of encouragement to. I stopped smiling, laughing, and existing. I stopped caring about the way I looked, about showering, about my dreams and what I still wanted from the world.

And, eventually, as I aimlessly scrubbed the same pan for the fifteenth time that day, Loss turned to me and said it was sorry. With an exasperated look upon its face, Loss said it had never meant for me to waste away, to sit staring at the walls of my house, wondering how I was ever supposed to go on with life. Loss explained to me that by stopping, all it had wanted was for me to breathe; but however unintentional, it had resulted in my failure to breathe life into my very existence.

So, I asked Loss, "What should we do now?"

And Loss moved toward me and opened its arms wide. "Come here," it said. So, I stepped into its arms in the same way a broken soul steps into sunlight for the first time. And Loss held me there for what seemed like longer than I had ever lived without it.

"Live with me," Loss said. "Breathe me in; hold me like I am holding you."

And after awhile, I began to feel Loss shrink, growing smaller and smaller, until it was I who was holding Loss.

THE FIRST HEARTBREAK

It's the first heartbreak
that stays with you.
Like old words in
a forgotten letter,
and the weather turning
colder in December,
it changes your heart forever.

In those moments, the pain
is like nothing you have felt before.
An immeasurable, unstoppable force,
as though you can't quite feel
your beautiful beating heart anymore.

The grief of losing a part of you
that would never ever be again.

And through the years, you will
often reflect on this first heartbreak
and how it shaped you in ways
you never thought it would,
and you will come to understand
however many ways it tried to
break you, it never could.

BROKEN THOUGHTS

A daydream or two
      hidden in a false smile
      and pretending as though
      everything is fine

Angry at the world
      and everything wrong
      feeling more alone
      as time goes on

There is no understanding
      for the things I feel
      nothing to truly see
      to help me begin to heal

That is the thing about life,
when you truly think about it.
I don't think anyone has the answer.
There is not one simple explanation to
make the universe make sense.

Instead, there are many answers
that will morph and change in the
same way the stars do over time
and the seasons do every year.

But if I have learned but a single
promising thing, it is that I have
never pursued an extraordinary life.

Instead, I have always strived
for a simple life, something so ordinary
some people might even think
it's a little dull.

But there are many wonderful
things about an ordinary life.

When you stop to smell
the carnations you have grown
in your garden yourself
or taste the passionfruit as it ripens
so marvelously in the spring.
When you cry over the things
you have lost and you laugh
over the things you have gained.

When holding hands is the most
intimate moment you can have with
someone you love so much.
When kindness rests firmly and
courageously in your heart,
and your most important goal
is to be a good friend.

And in all the simple things life
has to offer, and all the humility
that being ordinary brings,
I have found that this beautiful
and magical life is quite, in fact,

extraordinary.

Three weeks after my friend's brother died,
she finally left her bedroom.

We lay, stretched out on our backs,
in our favorite park.

"What does it feel like?" I asked her.

And she looked at me, with her beautiful green eyes
and sun-kissed nose, and pointed to the sky.
"The clouds, do you see them?"

"Yes."

"They're constantly moving and transforming.
This is what grief feels like. It will come and it will go,
never ending, but it will always change shape."

I can always tell
when the clock has stopped,
lost in time.

The hands stop ticking,
stagnant, paused, frozen.

But when I am lost,
it is not so easy.

I carry on, blindly, unable
to pinpoint the moment
I froze.

Beautiful people are
not just born,
they are shaped.

Beautiful are the people
who overcome struggle
and defeat.

Beautiful are the people
who put others before
themselves.

Beautiful are the people
who try to always have
encouraging things to say.

Beautiful are the people
who share their kindness
each and every day.

If I have learned anything
at all, it is that a beautiful
person reaches for you
every time you fall.

It is not always about how much
time it takes to reflect on the things
deep within our soul.

Some things cut so deep,
they feel as though they will never
heal at all.

As though the mere thought of them
is enough to send you into a perpetual
spiral of doubt and fear and
ongoing trauma.

But with reflection comes recovery.

And recovery is not measured on how
deep the cut or the wound or the scar.

The recovery is measured on the way
you adjust to living with the memory.

To understanding you will never be the
same again, and that is the point.

You're a new person, with another scar
in the story, but the scar does not define
the story.

LIGHT IN THE BOX

In a small town, far from any roads you or I would take, lived a young woman and her grandmother. As her grandmother grew older, she began to pass her lifelong lessons to her granddaughter, anticipating that she would carry these lessons into every life she would ever live. For a lesson, no matter how big or how small, is a lesson to carry with you, forever and more.

One day, while cleaning out the attic, the young woman found a box. A large wooden box with beautiful brass handles.

"What is this?" the woman asked her grandmother, who simply smiled in return and said, "Why don't you open it."

So, the young woman carefully unlocked the box and opened the lid, and out of the box spilled loss, grief, heartache, denial, shock, and light. The young woman, in horror, began reaching for all the pain and suffering, eager to stuff them back in the box where they belonged.

"Where is the light?" her grandmother asked.

"Who cares," the young woman replied. "Look at how big everything else is. It needs to be stopped."

Yet the grandmother did not focus on such things; instead, she reached for the light, and as she held it in her hands, it illuminated, beating, growing, and expanding around the attic, transforming loss, grief, heartache, denial, and shock into tiny specks of dust.

"The suffering will always be with us," the grandmother said. "But when we focus on the light, the suffering becomes smaller."

She passed the light to the young woman, who held the beating pulse in her hands, and said, "When we have light, the darkness is easier to live with, easier to manage."

TAKING STOCK

There once was a young boy who worked for his father at the corner store; he would stack shelves and take stock. His father had told him that taking stock was just about the most important thing in running the store. But over time, the boy became bored of taking stock, and so one day he decided simply not to do it.

And by not taking stock, it spared him at least an hour, and he was free to do as he pleased.

As it happened, on that same day, a young girl walked into the store, tired and frail, having had no sleep or any food for many days.

"Do you have some bread?" she asked the boy, and he nodded absentmindedly, pointing to the corner in which the bread was always kept.

The young girl disappeared only to return moments later. "I am sorry, but you don't have any bread."

Feeling annoyed, the boy went and looked himself. Sure enough, the young girl was telling the truth. He had not realized the bread had run out, and he had not ordered any more. So, the girl left the store, with no bread.

Embarrassed, the boy went home to tell his father what had happened. He explained that because he had not taken stock, the girl had not been able to buy any bread.

And his father looked at him. "Well, it is like life," he said. "If we do not take stock of our lives, if we do not reflect on our mistakes and how we can move forward, then we are unable to help others and much less ourselves."

Time Will Tell

Believe me when I say that I understand—
what it means to put every heart in your life
before your own.

The way you are pulled back and forth
like a pendulum, and, like time, it is constant.

As though you will never find a moment for
your own happiness—
for you are too consumed with the happiness
of all those you love.

Some days you are sad, and others you are angry—
how could it be that you put so much of
yourself on the line and get so little in return?

But I am learning, and perhaps you will too,
that it does not make your heart any less beautiful
if every now and then you say, "Not today;
today is just for me."

Sometimes I feel as though I need spares—a spare mind for the overflowing thoughts, a spare heart to store all the love I have to give, a spare soul for all these feelings. And I have often thought what life would be like if I had spare choices. If in the moments I had felt I'd made the wrong decision, I could choose the right one instead. But as life has taught me, every choice I've made has made me, me. Some decisions have been easy, and others have left me at a crossroad, not knowing which path to take. But every road has led me here, to who I am and who I know I can be. And so maybe life is about more than spare parts; maybe it's about taking the part that is broken and loving it anyway.

And I hope that
I can be a refuge—
that you see yourself
the way my eyes do,
that you hear your worth
in the sound of my voice,
that you feel at home
in my heart.

There is always room for the things we do not wish to feel, but even more for the things we need to feel. You will find it impossible to explain why, on some days, even just going to the grocery store feels like the world is ending; or, on some mornings, ordering coffee feels like every pair of eyes is looking at you, and they are whispering words of shame and judgment. You will struggle, trying to find the words to explain how difficult it is to get out of bed and get dressed, that you don't mean for the dishes to pile high or the laundry to go untouched for weeks on end.

You will hope, wish, and beg for someone to notice that this loss deep inside you takes more than words to comprehend. This shadow that follows your every footstep, this cloud that hangs over your heart, is not what defines you. So, in these unexplainable moments, when you cannot find the words, know that you deserve the world and all its kindness. Even in these moments, you will never be small or meaningless or worthless.

The Repairing

SEPTEMBER PALM

There is a palm tree in my garden.
It is as old as I can remember
it to be and has always been there,
reaching longingly for the sky.

One midafternoon, late September,
I noticed a ridge trailing down its trunk.
As though lightening had struck
the side and caused a great big scar.

And I couldn't understand
why I had never noticed before
this scar my tree wore.

I had wondered how often people
notice scars at all.

Because this scar didn't change how
beautiful the tree was to me,
or how much it belonged in my garden
for everyone to see.

FOREVER IN TIME

It was dusk, the sky a sweet lavender
a warm breeze rolling down the hills
of daffodils
swaying, magic in their soft dance
eternity spent in golden fields

She lay beside me, our faces
inches apart
her hand laced with mine
her laugh, a song in my heart

"Should we get going soon?"
I whispered into her hair
a stolen kiss as the light faded
the sky making way for the moon

"We have time," she said
"Yes," I replied
And time was resting in her eyes
I could look deep into those

forever

In the earliest part of dawn,
the curtain slightly drawn,
I awoke to a gleaming ray
of sunlight, still golden
from splitting the sky
between night and day.

And so, I reached to open
the curtain the whole way.

For every new day should
start with light.

The new day deserves
its stage as equally as the night.

I hit rock bottom when I no longer had any value for myself. I did not value my heart, my thoughts, my body, or my existence. Instead, I chose to belittle the one person who had always been there—me. I called her horrid names; I made her feel shame for the things she felt and guilt for the mistakes she had made. I looked at her day in and day out, and I told her she did not matter. "You'll never be like other women," I would say. "You will never be beautiful or interesting or strong." I would pick her apart, criticizing every little detail—her hair, her eyes, her nose, her lips, her body, her entire being—and I would convince her she was nothing.

Until, one day, I saw her as someone else entirely. I saw her as a friend, as someone I loved, as even a stranger I had just met. And when thinking of her like this, I was so ashamed of the hurt I could inflict. I realized I needed to earn her trust again, to remind her that she was valued and important and loved. And so I told her that while I had been a fire, angry and determined to burn everything to the ground, she had been the lantern. I promised to relearn what it meant to value her, and together we could light a path forward.

Time Will Tell

More than once in my life
I have been pressed for answers,
not knowing what to do,
what to say, or what thoughts
and feelings are valid.

And each time I am faced
with the things I cannot make
sense of, I understand healing
just a little bit more.

Healing doesn't always come
from the answers we seek
but the journey we take
in search of them.

I could pretend and tell you
that, long ago,
I finished recovering, that I
climbed mountains,
overcame challenges,
weathered storms,
arriving at the place of peace,
and I have since not left.

But this is not the truth,
because this is not life.
The truth of life
is finding recovery
in every new day.

Many months ago, I came into the care of some baby birds. These baby birds had been thrown from their nest, rejected and needing a new start.

They needed to heal slowly, relearn what it meant to live in the world, until they could grow strong enough to go back to the wild.

So, for weeks, I watched over the baby birds. Observing their slow and gradual learning, showing tenderness, and whispering words of encouragement.

When the fledglings were ready and subsequently released, I watched in admiration as they flew high into the late afternoon sky. Their strong wings beating, full of confidence, and I realized then that most of us are just like those baby birds.

We heal, grow, and repair ourselves when we are loved well. When we are shown care with no agenda, when we are encouraged by someone whose only goal is to see us return to the wild, better and stronger.

Over time, life had embroidered the ache into my skin, and to repair myself, the universe continued to insist that I unstitch myself, seam by seam.

"Why," I would sob into the night. "Why all the undoing?"

But the universe would not answer me.

Instead, it continued to hand me the needle, day after day, week after week, until every seam had been untangled and the stardust that made up my entire existence spilled out onto the floor.

"Why?" I repeated, angry, hurt, full of despair.

And the universe swept up all the stardust and blew it into the night air. Opened itself and handed me new stardust and new thread.

"Starting again," it said, "is the only way to repair."

To find growth is to communicate. You need to be able to say, "This is the way you made me feel; this is the way you hurt me." And whether you get the response you deserve, that is not so much the point. The point is having the courage to say, "I know my own heart, what it wants, needs, and deserves. And if you are not going to acknowledge my heart and validate the things that I feel, then you will not have a place in my heart to stay."

There will be a time in your life when your heart will shatter, and it will take everything to repair it. You will hold strong for a while, refuse to let the walls come down, because allowing anyone to see us break is a thought not many of us can bear. You will put on a brave face; you will smile through the pain; you will tell the people you love you are doing okay and find comfort in strangers because the surface will be easier to manage. You will tell yourself every day not to cry, because crying will make the ache so much more real.

But sooner or later the release will come. And whether it be in the car, in the shower, in the grocery store line, in front of strangers or your best friend, you will sob. You will sob so hard your lungs will feel as though they are no longer with you, that they are somewhere else, detached from you. And you will want to disappear, to go somewhere warm and filled with light, somewhere you can breathe.

But it is in this moment, through the unrelenting tears, you will know you are still alive. Still feeling and still holding on.

So, in this moment, when it feels as though you cannot breathe, just know that the tears will dry, the ache will go, and you will know what it means to survive.

One night, I had a dream about a forgotten cottage at the end of a very long path in the middle of a very large forest. And inside the cottage were aching memories and difficult thoughts. The owner of the cottage had piled all their deepest, darkest moments inside and left the cottage to fade away and become overgrown with weeds and wildflowers. So, I began to mend the holes in the walls and sweep away the dust; I tended to the garden and planted daisies all along the path. I whispered to the cottage that it was not measured by all its mistakes in the past. Over time, the cottage began to glow and sing inside. It felt warm and magical and full of hope. Because while we try to ignore our darkness, we should remember that for a new chapter to begin, we must first allow the light back in.

I have had many years
of not understanding,
of not knowing
what to call this loss.

How do you lose
something or someone
that was never yours
to begin with?

How do I grieve
when I never *had?*

How do I repair
what never really *was?*

No one chooses
the way you mend
the things that
another broke.

No one tells you
the way you put
yourself
back together again.

It's an amazing thing
to have a mind
that is its own universe—
filled with endless possibility.
There is no shame in taking
time to process grief or anger
or difficulty.
Your mind has every right
to protect itself.

We met in a park, not long
after the start of the new year.

You were every breath of fresh air,
and quickly we became two stars
colliding, two hearts locked together
in a dare.

But I remember laughing
one late evening, and I asked,

"Where have you been all my life;
how did you get here?"

So, you described every dark corner,
shadow, and road you had taken up
until this point in your journey.

Every moment and memory had all
led you to the light.

And you swept yourself against me,
hands either side of my face,
and you said, "It's you.
You are the light."

Even in the darkest moments
of your entire life, when nothing
feels like it will lead you home,
when life is burning, collapsing,
and slipping away, you must hold on
to the tiniest flicker of strength,
for it is there, in the smallest ounce
of hope, that you will understand
the true nature of your soul
and your will to fight.

THE MARATHON

A group of runners set out one morning along a fire trail. One foot in front of the other, each determined not to fail.

One runner stopped at each checkpoint, made themself a cup of tea, and reminded their heart to breathe. The other runners laughed and did not stop. "You will lose," they jeered. "You are weak," they taunted.

But the one runner did not listen and continued to stop at each checkpoint.

So, on and on the runners went, until the very end, when the one runner came toward the finish line and saw the others hunched over, having never finished the race, despite running all day long.

As the runner crossed the line, winning the race, they turned to the others. "Life is not a sprint," they said, smiling. "It's a marathon."

A ROOM OF DOORWAYS

Let me tell you the story of the woman
and a room filled with doorways.

There was once a room filled with doorways—
each door a different color but with no signage.
There was no clear way of telling where the
speckled doorway led, or the pale-blue door,
or the door covered in wildflowers.

Even so, the woman went on to turn the handles
and open the doors. By opening some of the doors,
the woman was met with pain, sadness, and doubt.
But by opening other doors, she was met with joy,
light, and hope.

So, on and on she went, opening each
and every door for what seemed like eternity—
never really knowing what lay beyond
and yet always with a burning desire to continue
opening each door.

Until, one day, after growing a little older, and
becoming a little wiser, the woman realized that
the doors all had something in common—
for every door she opened, no matter the feeling
she stepped into, she could always see the dawn beyond.

Every door had a silver lining.

And, so, this is what the woman learned—
that light was found in the spaces of every door.
For no matter the despair and struggle in life,
there is always light at the end of every corridor.

The moon whispered
into my dreams one day,
"When I say I am here,
I don't mean I am here
out of habit.

"I mean I am here
because your face
in my reflection
is the most beautiful thing
about this planet."

It was knowing you
that taught me someone
could break my heart
in exactly the same place
time and time again.

But also it was knowing you
that taught me I could
restore it, and my heart
became stronger
and stronger until I
walked away.

Every person I lost, whether it was a lover or a friend, left a hole inside me that no amount of fresh soil could ever fill.

There was the person who I shared all my plans with; my biggest joys and successes; and my deepest, darkest secrets.

I couldn't call and share what I had stumbled upon that made me laugh, finding something I thought they would enjoy. The right was no longer mine; the cord had been cut; the dial tone gone.

So, I chose to share these things with myself, instead, pull the soil from different parts of my body, and fill the hole in my heart with my own light. And this did not mean that I did not want to share all of these things one day with someone else; it just meant, for the time being, I was learning to love myself.

You are going to live a life full of ups and downs. You are not going to be able to control everything that happens to you. You are going to laugh and cry and really laugh and really cry. You are going to be exhausted by some moments and filled with excitement and joy in others. You are going to walk some paths alone and others hand in hand with someone who cares. You are going to climb mountains and shoot for the stars, and on both you may fall, but you must continue forward anyway. You are going to learn that you only have one life to live, so live it well.

Your dignity still exists in the
moments when you are overwhelmed.

Life knows that it is not easy.

It doesn't matter if the things that
overwhelm you do not overwhelm
other people—
they are still worthy of grace.

We all respond to things differently.

We are stressed, frustrated, and annoyed
by different things.

This does not give someone else the
right to deny what you feel or your
capacity to process these emotions.

People have different triggers—
their need to release is their own.

There are always going to be people in the world who judge others and judge you. Sometimes, they will be woven into your life, and it'll be impossible to untangle yourself. Maybe they will be someone you work with, part of your family, a lover, a friend, a person who is tied to you—even if you don't want them to be. People will tell you "just leave" or "just remove them from your life," as though it's that simple; it's not always that black-and-white. Gray exists in the fabric of our relationships with people. The most important thing you can do is understand that you are more than the judgment. It is not a reflection of you but them. Understand that this person doesn't get to control your emotions; you do.

I am hurt.

There is nothing beautiful about the person you love hurting you. It aches. It sits in your chest. You can't eat or sleep or concentrate on anything other than the pain you feel.

I am sad.

There is nothing magical about the person you love making you sad. You feel it in your bones. You can't move, can't see the wonder of life. All you can think about is that you want the running thoughts to stop.

But I deserve better. I know I do. I don't deserve to be hurt or to be sad.

Of all the things I have ever done, I know that I deserve to be treated like I am the sun.

I am uncertain of the road to take back—
the way you love me feels different.

How do I trust the words that you say,
fold them around my heart and let them stay?

There is a piece inside me, now broken,
thrown somewhere out into the wide-open sky,
and I have no ability to fly.

But perhaps it is not about the road behind
but the road in front.

If you take my hand, and I take yours,
if you take my wings and I take yours,
then together we can search the skies;
together we can turn our love
back into fireworks.

For a while, I felt anger linger
in all the spaces of my heart—
and I could not understand why
I felt such anger all the time.

I was angry at the world,
angry for the things
I could not control,
angry for the hurt that I felt
every moment of every day.

Then one day, late into the evening,
when the moon had risen and the
cicadas played a melody
outside my window,
Anger appeared in my living room.

And I asked, "Why are you here,
tormenting me, crushing the life
right out of me?"

And Anger replied,
"Because I remind you of all the
things you will not tolerate.
I am here because you know
you deserve more."

I looked for ways to heal,
in all the things I thought
might be good to try to do.

I tried many things, like yoga
and walking forgotten trails,
like flower pressing and coffee
classes, and digging my toes
into the sand.

I tried baking and gardening and
lying out in the sun; I tried book
clubs and journaling and anything I
thought might be fun.

And it wasn't until a gray sort of day,
when I didn't feel like trying
much of anything, that someone
I loved turned to me, with a look that
was earnest and true, and simply said,
"Darling, why don't you just try to be you."

A STORY OF TWO OAK TREES

In an old park, just down the road, there were two oak trees.

One tree refused to feel, too afraid to allow life to seep into the roots, for it would mean feeling things too deeply. And so the tree began to rot; fungi broke down the wood within the tree, and it weakened, splitting and decaying.

But the second tree felt the world around it, and it allowed life to seep deep into its roots, feeling everything that life brought its way. And so it grew, taller and taller, with branches that reached for the sun, sprouting flowers and fruits, becoming home to many brightly colored birds.

I think of these trees often, and especially of the tree that grew.

For its true message was simple—we grow by letting life in.

So, tell the people you love how you feel, be sensitive and vulnerable, and feel deeply. Understand that while life can be dark, it can also be wonderful. Feel things in every moment—the joy, the ache, the wonder, and the disappointment.

And all of it will help you to grow.

There is more to resilience than starting again.

We start again every day.

We can recover after everything that knocks us down.
But resilience takes understanding, to know that we
will carry our strength every day for the rest of our lives.

That if one thing breaks us, another thing will too,
but we must keep going.

Resilience is sailing into a storm knowing that the thunder
will roar and the lightening will strike, knowing that the ship
will be pummeled and thrashed about but that it is not going
to drown you.

Whatever the damage, you will survive it, and you will do it
while navigating your way out of the storm.

The Change

All the leaps and bounds
of change and the like
are never a simple thing
or happen overnight.

But perhaps if we embraced
the idea that we can do better,
that the earth needs us united,
now more than ever—

then we would suffer a little less
corruption, pollution, and falsity
and thrive with a little more
fairness, hope, and true equality.

When you have known something
your whole life, it will be frightening
to accept that the path may change.

But you have to be willing to evolve
and open your mind to endless possibilities.

The snow covers the ground, and the
earth falls into the deepest slumber,
but eventually the snow melts away
and wildflowers return with wonder.

The clouds blanket the day in gray,
hiding the sun and all its warmth,
but skies do clear, and so does our fear.

The leaves fall, and when they return,
they are never truly the same,
but they still return, each one more
beautiful than the season before.

There is a process to accepting
that we cannot always achieve
everything we set out to do.

That change does not happen
by simply willing it to come true;
it takes courage and strength
and a willingness to carry on,
to move forward through every
bump and hurdle.

The undeniable truth of change
is that nothing in life ever
stays the same, but the power
in this truth, despite all the moments
we question why,
is that to fail is to fly.

Deep in the woods, underneath thick canopies and undergrowth, a small village existed—and in the village lived an owl and a fox. Life was as it had always been, day by day, night by night, the sun would rise and set.

But one day, a terrible fire swept through the forest; it engulfed many beautiful things, leaving ash and ruin in its wake.

Fox came to Owl, tears welling in her eyes. "I have lost everything," Fox said. "I do not know where to begin again."

And Owl said, "You are not alone; many must rebuild."

"How," said Fox, "when my home is all but ash and rubble?"

"We cannot change what has happened," said Owl, "only what way we look forward."

"But so much of who I am is in the past," replied Fox.

"Yes," said Owl, "but you are focused on all the rubble."

And Owl pointed toward the ruin of Fox's home. "You are not seeing the heart of the matter. Of what it means to change."

And, sure enough, in the center of the rubble, a tiny sprout was growing toward the sun.

I understand it because I feel it too. Something happens, and it forces you to change. And this battle ensues day by day, night by night. You wrestle with who you were and who you are becoming. And you feel so alone—even if you are surrounded, you still feel alone. You grow tired of always talking about it, wanting to release it but not wanting to burden those around you. So, the ache sits on your chest, wrapped so tightly around your heart, every breath hurts. You're dazed while the world goes on. People still have joy, but you can't see it. You can't see joy in anything, and you don't know why. You want to talk about it, find the words to explain it, but you can't. There are no words, only this unrelenting feeling. It feels like it will never go away, that it will stay forever. But feelings come and go, as surely as the tide is pulled in and away from the shore. To live with such change is to accept that, despite how rough the seas can be, the calmness always returns.

At some point, you are going to learn that life is not perfect. You can choose happiness each day, but there will be days where the sun does not shine, and this is okay. You can experience all your dreams coming true only to decide you want new dreams, and this is okay. You can give all that you've got, and it is suddenly and unexpectedly taken away from you, and this is okay. You don't wait for the flowers to bloom around you; you water them and watch them grow. You build your home, brick by brick, layer by layer, and you weather the rust, the grit, and the broken windows. And you realize, no matter how many times life changes course or how many moments you fall, it is you who plants your roots firmly into the ground and continues the walk. This is the place of realization, where beauty is born—where the ordinary becomes the extraordinary.

It was always us against the world.
But we've changed.
It feels like I am upside down.
I can't see things clearly.

There's too much rain and not enough sun.

Is it broken now?

little love, where do we go from here
I know we can't pretend
seems like we've lost our way
I hope this is not the end

feels like we've drifted away
and there is no light
to see you in the dark
but I am hoping you will stay

little love, where do we go from here
I know we can't pretend
seems like we've lost our way
I hope this is not the end

is it worth it—all this love we share
the life we made together
the dreams that all came true
do you still know how much I care

little love, where do we go from here
I know we can't pretend
seems like we've lost our way
I hope this is not the end

maybe we can start again
my heart still chooses you
I can't lose my best friend
I hope this is not the end
I hope this is not the end

THE WAY MY BODY CHANGED

So many people would look at me
and say, "You look so good. How much
weight have you lost?"

So many people would stop me
and ask, "What's the magic answer?
I'll do whatever it costs."

So many people would lean in, and,
like a secret only we knew, they would
whisper to me, "I wish I could do that too."

But the answers were never found
in those numbers on my scale—
the meaning of "healthy" was less
about what I looked like and more
what it meant to me, not to fail.

A journey is a journey and can be
written in so many different ways,
and your body should be loved—
every atom, every cell, and every nerve,
praised like it truly deserves.

For the real work started on the day
I looked into the mirror and said—
"No mountain is too high or river too far.
No matter the reflection we see,
I love you as you are."

It took years to value my self-worth,
and there are still those moments,
however—fleeting some months
or enduring the next—when I question
my place here on this earth.

But on those days, I would look upward
and seek out the beauty of the moon—
how she would remind me of my voice
and all the ways that it can soar.

How she would tell me to open my lungs
and howl every dark thought into the sky—

just like the wolf when the moon is high.

We orbit change—
we begin by reaching
toward the sky,
and then we spend
many moons flying,
only to shrink again
and return to the soil.
And from the earth
grows new life.
So, if you find yourself
in times of struggle,
remember that change
is an everlasting cycle.

It isn't the simplest lesson to learn—that some people will never truly understand you. That you could set up as many boundaries as possible and there will always be someone who doesn't honor those boundaries. It has taken so many breaths to learn that some people will just never understand the way I move through the world—how some days it's too hard to talk on the phone, that I lose my way in a crowd, that knowing I cannot fix everything creates an ache. But in the same breaths, I have also learned that there are people who *do* understand. These are the people I hold on to, the people who understand the language my heart speaks, who don't judge the thoughts I have or the things I feel. And so, I have learned a more important lesson—that life is not about begging people to understand you but celebrating who you already are.

All beautiful things start from within, like taking your first steps and climbing your first jungle gym. It doesn't matter from where you derive your strength—poetry or music, hiking trails or sunsets, campfires or taking a deep breath. There are days we were never warned about, when an ache takes residence in your heart and sadness fills you up to the brim, where all that overflows is a sense of doubt, as though you can no longer win. We were never taught that within the wreckage exists change. That in order to become the phoenix, you must accept the ash. Here's to giving your soul permission to start again. Here's to allowing your heart the chance to start over. Here's to reminding your mind that, while it can be frightening, taking a leap is as powerful as lightning.

It has been an uphill battle, to watch you through this transition—of realizing that one dream was not the one that fulfilled you and not knowing what to do with this. The fear inside you unstitching the very fabric you had woven your life into. But I have also seen the strength it took, to take in the deepest breath of your life and exhale to start again.

So, know this: for every change you cycle through, and how it changes life and us, I will still stand beside you, embracing every moment, day by day. Because the vow we made together was that life is beautiful, not because of what comes our way but because navigating every storm together is what we have promised, forever and ever.

I wish you strength on all your journeys—from the ones that bring you joy to the ones that force you to look fear in the eyes and continue forward. I wish you laughter in the moments that press against your heart and make it ache. I wish you patience to understand your needs and wants and desires. I wish you perspective when life feels a little cloudy. I wish you humility when reflecting on the things in your life you wish to change. I wish you courage to accept that the things that change inside of you will always shape the things around you.

When we arrive in the world, we are already born into change—and we spend a lifetime growing, evolving, and fluctuating. Our hair changes, our cells replenish, our hearts experience love and loss, our minds gain new perspectives. Our bones break and heal, our bodies weather storms, our skin bruises and wears scars of stories. But perhaps it is our soul that bares the most change. The way it lights up in times of beauty or struggles in times of despair. But it is also our soul that learns. Despite all the things that will change and evolve around you, you are who you are because the world decided it needed you.

You need to fail more than once in life, to know that this is what makes you grow. Believe me, I know how frightening failure can be. I have shot my shot and missed—dozens of times. I have sought assistance and instead received no reply. I have written pages and thrown them away. I have battled with continuing on, preferring to trade it all in for a better day. But in all my failures was an important lesson—I am my own maker. I decide how fast I run and how far I travel. I decide how high I jump and how much I carry. A new perspective arrived on the day I made room for failure, knowing that for every time I fail, another rung is added to a ladder, encouraging me to climb.

You shouldn't rewrite the steps
you have taken or undo the stitches
you have woven.

Every step leads you along the path
to where you arrive every day,
and all the stitches sew together
the person you are becoming.

It may be bold to say
but necessary to be honest—
you can either stay stagnant
and unchanged
or you can keep moving
toward evolving.

We often face challenges
and routines that feel as though
they are repeating, as though
we have been here before and
cannot go through the
same things again.

You need to remind yourself
of what you will and won't accept
and hold dear the love
you give yourself
on such path of change.

I too have known the resistance
to change.

But something that has taken me
a long time to know is this—
the change does not happen
in the waiting but in the living.

When you are on the brink
of telling the world who you are,
the fear that everything will change
is real.

Not wanting people to see you
or treat you differently is a valid fear.

And you'll ask yourself time and time again,
What does my life mean to others?
Who am I to the people I love?

But perhaps it is more important to ask,
Am I moving through the world
in the way I want to?
Am I loving in the way I was born to?

You will be ready when you are ready,
but know this—
you deserve recognition, validation,
and a road to walk that is steady.

I met Change in an airport once; I had one suitcase packed, with the thought of running away. Life had become unstable, too difficult to find the will to continue in all the mess. Change had considered my packed bags and thoughtfully offered, "You are running because you are afraid of the things you cannot see."

"That's the point," I had replied. "I am comfortable on the road I have been on, always knowing what is around every bend."

And Change said to me, "What you have known is a familiar path. You have laid the path yourself, stone by stone. You know the shape, the color, and the texture of each stone you have laid. To place your foot on each stone, one after the other, feels comfortable. But the road is plain. There are no longer any flowers that grow in between the cracks. No longer any bursts of breeze that make you feel alive."

And believe me, I had wanted to continue running; turning away was better than facing change itself.

But Change reassured me, "I will walk with you, and together we will lay new stones; together we will find new flowers growing. Together we will know what it means to be alive."

I live at the bottom of a mountain.

The sun rises and sets on either side,
and it is beautiful.

The trees reach for the sky; there are always
birds circling the tallest peaks.
You can see the ocean from the top,
stretched out for miles, as far as the eye can see.

Every dawn and dusk, the fog rolls in.

It is thick and heavy and covers the mountain
and the passage I take up and down.

I was once afraid of the fog—frightened of the
shadows that were not visible to me.

But I know better now.

The fog lifts.

I used to believe choices were black and white, right or wrong. But, lately, I have been admiring what it means to live in the gray. To know that we are never the same as we were yesterday or last week or every year that goes by. And I suppose it is curious, the way life falls apart and creates new pieces, and with these pieces we construct new mosaics. I am always painting, and often the strokes are all different, but that is the beauty—we are never the same one moment to the next.

Striving to evolve means that we can become so invested in being better that we miss all the things that make us who we are today. We wait for change to arrive in a grand entrance, often marking such change with big transformations like birthdays and anniversaries and new year resolutions. But we miss all the little moments, all the smaller pieces that have melded together to create the bigger picture—like a warm shower after being caught in the rain, the sweetness of strawberries on a summer day, setting foot in a city we've never been to, chocolate melting in our mouths, knowing we have a few extra minutes in bed, and finishing the best book we've ever read. If we celebrate all the little things that bring us joy each day, then we find the courage in our hearts to continue on our way.

It has taken me almost my whole life to be at peace with my solitude. To spend time with myself, to get to know me—and who I want to be as a friend, a partner, a person, a soul of the universe. And when I sat with myself and all the things I felt and all the ways I wanted to move through the world, I learned what I would and would not stand for. It can be challenging to set boundaries with people. To tell them, "The way you treat me is not the way I deserve to be treated." But it is necessary to draw these lines.

There was once a time machine built by a magician and left in a field of dandelions. Two small dandelions began to use the time machine, hoping to find answers to the questions they'd had all their lives. The first dandelion used the time machine to revisit the past each day. They relived every mistake and every moment, poring over each memory. They analyzed every step and how they could have changed the outcome. Eventually, the dandelion became stuck in the past, unable to move on. The second dandelion, however, only used the time machine to look back at the past fondly, to recount the lessons they had learned and to move forward. The past is important, for it gives you the tools to build a future, but the present gives you moments to create the memories you'll carry forever.

The little flower
pulled in all the
elements to grow—
the soil, the sun, the rain.

For it knew, the things
that give us life
are often the very things
that encourage us to change.

To write was all I knew.

It was calming, therapeutic, healing.

But, over time, the writing became my role.

It was a responsibility I had to the people
who were reading these words.

And so, the therapy, the healing, the calm
began to ebb away.

And it was crushing.

What would I do if I could not find solace
in words?

So I looked to other things—
walking, moving, breathing.

This is the same for you.

There are many things that can heal you.

Do not be afraid when this changes—
when life hands you different things
to help you grow.

All the photos
hung up on your wall
tell a story of how
far you've traveled
and while in some seasons
you may fall
and the pictures
can appear to unravel—
notice the smaller details
within the frames
the way the light
in your eyes remains
for even if the pictures
constantly change
the wonder of who you are
stays the same

This is what it means to be with someone, for all your life—time changes you, both individually and who you become to each other. What was once a spark evolves into something much deeper, filling a fireplace with flames to keep you warmer. And when you walk through each chapter, writing your tale, knowing that every chapter will be different gives you perspective. It is not always about every line, paragraph, and page but the beauty of the whole story.

How do I convey
with so little words
that everything in your life
will eventually be okay?

I think of you
and my heart feels joy.

I look at you
and my soul knows hope.

I am in awe of you
and all the things you can do.

Sometimes, the things you set your heart on won't happen. You are going to have many things, in fact, that don't go your way. And it will hurt. You will wonder why the person you loved could not love you in the same way, or why the friend you needed suddenly turned away, or why the book or article or video you spent hours and hours working on never got the recognition you thought it would. You will wonder why the path you took led to a dead end or why the journey had so many unanswered questions, too difficult to comprehend. But during the hurt, you will learn things. You will learn to see the balance between pain and happiness and that, often, one cannot exist without the other.

You will learn that balance and acceptance are key ingredients to help a heart recover. You will learn that success is not truly measured by others but by yourself and every goal you set and meet, and despite every setback or day that doesn't go your way, none of it makes you any less and none of it makes you weak. You will learn that being kinder to yourself has as much beauty as the sky and all its color and, above everything, the universe will always think you are a wonder.

The Awakening

There is a voice
inside you
that grows stronger
with every breath.

It says to you—
for all the times
you have tried to fit in,
there are more times
the world has wished
for you to love the person
you already are.

The stars encourage you
to awaken all the strength
within your heart
and lead your life
in the way
you were born to
from the start.

The most beautiful thing you can do is hold out your hand when someone falls. The most beautiful thing you can do is listen when someone talks about their fears and insecurities, to remind them that their flaws do not define them or diminish their capabilities. The most beautiful thing you can do is to show empathy, for you do not know what battles people may face day-to-day. The most beautiful thing you can do is lift up someone's spirits, for joy always keeps the darkness away. The most beautiful thing you can do is laugh and dance for all of time. The most beautiful thing you can do is hold on to your dreams and always be kind.

Five things we should say
as a reminder to the people we love

I.
You are the sunlight worth starting every day for.

II.
There are not enough moments to tell you
how much you mean to me.

III.
Your laugh makes all my troubles fade away.

IV.
You are not defined by your mistakes,
and I'll always stand by you.

V.
You are the moonlight that brightens
the sky every night.

There will be many times in life when you will look back and you will wonder if you could have changed what happened. You will wonder what else could have been done or if only you had murmured all the words on the tip of your tongue. But you cannot change the path you have already walked; you cannot erase the steps you have already taken; you can only change the path ahead of you and the steps yet to come. It is here; as you mold a new path, your mind awakens.

Life had been going well—there were more good days than there were bad. But yours was difficult. Your heart had been broken and, even though I listened, there was nothing I could really say or do to make you see all the things I could see, that you would find happiness again, that love would return to your heart.

It wasn't until things in my life turned a little upside down too that I finally knew what you meant when you had said there were days you went to sleep and wished you didn't have to wake up. That all you wanted was for the running river of thoughts to dry out, for all your feelings to shrivel into nothingness, the world to turn quiet.

But I could also see how far you had traveled, that your darkness was subsiding, that you had found the light again.

And this gave me hope—for I knew if you could survive, I could too.

This is what it means to be human—we think other people's happiness is our responsibility. There was a time when I was the pillar for everyone. I was the listener, the supporter, and the one lending my arms to carry all the people in my life whom I loved. But, over time, I was pulled from every direction. It felt like I was being split in a million different pieces and what was left over was just a shell of whom I knew myself to be. The real understanding came when I finally understood that it was not up to me to carry everyone else.

There was a time
when so many things
went wrong, and I was
angry at the world.

I asked time and time again—
"Why are you doing this to me?
Why can't I achieve these things?
Why don't I have what I want?"

But I had been so focused on
all the things I did not have
I had forgotten to focus
on all the things I *did* have.

This was a moment of clarity—

I told my heart the world beats
at my feet, waiting for me to dance.

I told my mind success comes
in many smaller moments.

I told my soul desire is often
a current, always changing.

It is not always about the
things we wish for or hope for
or spend years chasing after.
Instead, it is finding solace
in all the things we *already* have.

We often hibernate—
we are awoken to new ideas
and new possibilities
that eventually become
another routine,
so we close our eyes,
only to find that we need
to reawaken again.

It's a continuous cycle.

But there is always joy in
awakening again.

It reminds us that we are
still here, still alive—
like a good pair of jeans
or the start of spring,
like your favorite sweater
or the bird outside your window
returning each week to sing.

Despite everything, there will be someone you leave behind. They'll be gone, and you'll be different. You'll remember the summer you sat out on the porch drinking champagne and the night glowed with fireflies and your stomach felt full and warm. Those sunsets, filled with laughter as you chased each other through the sand and foam-washed shoreline, thinking that life couldn't get any better than that. And maybe you'll always wonder if life had only gone the way you had planned, but sometimes life changes course—and this is probably the hardest thing you'll ever have to understand.

It was three thirty in the morning,
and I awoke, reaching across
the empty space in my bed.

And I thought that you might
be there—folded into my arms,
but you weren't, and it hurt.

I have lived to know the pattern
of your breathing and the gentle
sounds you make in your sleep.

I have survived in the memory
of how your skin feels against mine.

It's three thirty in the morning,
and it's taking everything to go
back to sleep—because you aren't here.

I wish you were here.

Time Will Tell

If you are honest,
you will acknowledge
that there are days
the mirror hurts.

Sometimes your hair
is messy, your eyes
a little swollen,
your smile small.

You will tell yourself—
I am beautiful.
But the day is filled
with dread and sorrow,
so your heart won't
trust the words you speak.

And on these days,
when you are hoping
to be somebody else,
remind yourself even in
all the quiet—
you are here because
life would not be as
wonderful without you.

THE SUGAR GLIDERS

It was the first time I had planted my roots in a home that had captured my heart, and there had been an old tree. It towered in the yard, filled with disease and rotten wood. The tree had died long ago. Eventually, I knew it needed to go, and so the loppers came, cutting the tree down, piece by piece. As the tree was being dismantled, a small family of sugar gliders emerged from inside the hollow. They scurried from the rotten bark to other trees in my yard. After the tree was gone, I woke up each morning and felt guilt. For while the tree had died, it had still been a home to these small creatures.

One dusk, as the sun sank behind the mountain, I ventured into my yard to pick the ripened fruit growing on an apple tree. And sure enough, in the canopy above me, I spotted the sugar gliders, pairs of little eyes staring down at me from between the branches and bark.

They had made a new home.

Now, each time my life becomes difficult, I think of those sugar gliders, for they had made me realize, even when things fall apart, we can find sanctuary in new beginnings.

You cannot outrun yourself. It does not matter how many twists and turns or times you try to hide, every moment will always catch up to you. So, my advice is this—dive right in. Even if the pain is too difficult to look at head-on, even if you feel there is not enough time to unbox all the things you feel, do it anyway. We are told to smother pain, to fill up the holes in our hearts with ash and dust and walk the other way. But even if the sky blankets the forest in snow, the wildflowers will still find a way to grow. So too will pain.

I have known insecurity,
and I have attached myself
to the what-ifs, a lot.

What if the sun did not shine
or the rivers did not flow?
What if I missed my flight,
or became lost in the snow,
or time moved too slow?
What if I made too many mistakes
or could not learn to exhale and let go?

The things I could control made me
feel safe—at home in my heart.
When I knew the course of the ship,
I was never afraid to sail.

But I have since come to know,
the ocean moves in different directions—
the waves, the wind, the tide.

So, I could spend my life worried
about what-ifs and the like,
or I could embrace the unknown—
and all the wonder of life.

You never forget the people in your corner. The ones who lift you up when you are spiraling out of control, the people who hold out their arms when you need to fall, the souls that say I am here, and it's powerful because of the meaning it holds. And for all the times in your life when you take them for granted, because it is an easy thing to do, there are also some mornings when you rise, and the day is bright, and you have this profound realization that the sun is brought home to you by the people who love you.

I once heard
that if a lady beetle
landed on your shoulder,
let her fly and make a wish.

But, over time, I began to wish
for her.

Fly high, soak in all the world
around you, be free and wild and alive.

It dawned on her one day
that she was not to be loved
piece by piece.

That the love she deserved
was to be loved for all
that she was.

I realized then
that life was never
not going to change.

The world itself
turns on an axis,
always leaving us
a little off-balance.

But this doesn't define
our ability to orbit the sun.

I have often wondered
why we apologize for things
that are out of our control.

I am sorry I am feeling unwell,
I am sorry the sun isn't shining today,
I am sorry my train was late,
I am sorry for feeling this way,
I am sorry for someone else's mistakes.

I'm sorry.
I'm sorry.
I'm sorry.

And, as I've grown a little older,
I've spent less time apologizing
for the things I cannot control,
understanding that, in life,
sometimes
all it takes is the strength to let go.

I open the door
there you are in the dark
all on your own
trying to find your spark

Lonely heart
how did you forget your light
seems like you gave it all away
please don't cry tonight

Remember what you said to me
strength never fades away
just takes so much time to see

Lonely heart
how did you forget your light
seems like you gave it all away
please don't cry tonight

You'll rise beyond this night
everything will be all right

Lonely heart
how did you forget your light
seems like you gave it all away
please don't cry tonight

Everything will be all right
Everything will be all right

Time Will Tell

I have spent so many days
worrying about other people—
if they will understand me,
notice me, offer a hand or kind
words on my journey to belonging.

But the person I should have spent
all those days with was myself.

I should have asked her,
*How do you want to move through
the world? Do you see the stars
in your sleep, how they emit light
just for you? Do you know that
every step you take is another step
toward becoming?*

So, I offer some simple advice—
make this life about you.

There has been a void deep inside my heart, for many winters. I learned to exist within the void, to understand its wants and desires, searching for the magic in its mystical opalescence. But, this year, the springtime was different than the others, filled with marigolds and lavender and little honeybees in the garden—beautiful wonders—and perhaps the beauty allowed me to understand what my heart had always known to be true; your worth does not depend on whether other people choose to see you.

You are still beautiful,
even if you wear
one hundred scars.

You are still beautiful,
even if you are still
on your way.

You are still beautiful,
in every moment
of every day.

I know this feeling
of gentle revival

> to have awoken suddenly
> from a long and profound slumber

> there is no more suffering
> for the suffering has slept

this flood of feeling, of perception—
of knowing bluebirds fly again
and little flowers repollinate the forest

the need to sleep and reawaken—
a constant, everlasting cycle

> always new beginnings

And there we were,
singing the lyrics
to our favorite song,
in a stadium of
twinkling lights,
feeling like we really
belonged—
and even in a sea of others,
your smile lit up the night.
I knew then that my love for you
was brighter than any color.

You used to run without taking a second glance or barely needing a breath; you used to climb trees and jump off waterfalls; you used to recognize little details without needing to look closer. Now, you need an extra moment before getting out of bed; a nice cup of tea will soothe your soul; each step a little more cautious, so that the ground beneath you is steady. And if all you know yourself to be are the things you have always done, if you wake up one day and you aren't those things anymore, you wonder if this makes you less of the person you were the day before. But this is what happens—time. We are so afraid of time going by, of turning the pages in our life, and suddenly another chapter has ended. But you know things now that you did not know in the chapters before. That a broken heart doesn't mean the end, that those few extra minutes in bed can bring all the joy you need for the day ahead. There may no longer be leaping and bounding and chasing every breath, but you gain something so much more as life continues on—like awareness and understanding and a little more depth.

I am sure you are much like me—you have listed your expectations of life and tried to remain steadfast in it all coming true. You have built scenarios and situations in the library that exists within your mind, and when any of them falter or change course, it is as though the library has collapsed on top of you. There you are, in the darkness and debris, angry that the things you had hoped for did not go your way. And yet, the darkness always teaches us something—the shadows dance—and even in such obscurity, we discover new thoughts. It is here we are reminded that life is both beautiful and awful, and in between live all the moments we had planned and all the moments that had not gone to such plan—but the story can live on, and so too the library.

The time I took for myself
taught me a lot of things—

That the road to self-discovery
is neither clean nor a direct path.
That I can continue to rediscover
what it means to be this soul,
living in this body, part of this
world and existing in this life.

I learned to look inward, beyond
all the challenges and murky waters.
I learned to dive deeper, to uncover
all the fragments of my soul
and to surrender to such grace.

The dawn returns, and we rise,
with another chance to let go
all the feelings we suppress.
We awaken each new day,
to carry on through the process.

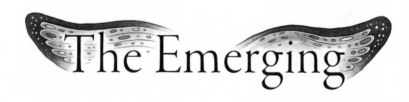

The Emerging

The transformation takes time;
it will be uncomfortable.

Your limits will be tested.
Your worth will be challenged.
Your faith will be questioned.

But you will emerge
stronger, kinder, more patient
than how you entered.

I know the world struggles, and I know that it can be harsh and horrid and cruel. But I also know that it can be compassionate and bright and kind. This is why, for every path I walk and every person I meet, I will show them light. I know that I am not perfect; I know that there are always things I can do better and ways I can be better. But I will continue to try. I will not let my heart turn cold, I will not apologize for feeling deeply or being soft, I will always express gratitude and mindfulness, and I will never give up on kindness.

I once knew someone who did not leave
the house for nearly a year.
The door was locked, the windows closed,
and the curtains drawn.
Every day, I would walk by the house,
hoping to see life emerge, and yet for
all the days the life remained inside,
I stayed hopeful.

I did not give up on them, and I never
once believed they would not emerge
into the world once more—
when they were ready.

And they did emerge.

Now, they are out again in the world,
and they're the best they've ever been.

Some moths stay cocooned for weeks,
months, or years—you cannot rush
someone's process and how they choose
to heal from all their deepest thoughts and fears.

You will always be someone I wish good things for. I have watched your soul grow, even in the moments as you planted your roots and sank deep into the soil, only to rise stronger than ever before. I have admired your courage; I have seen the way your smile rivals a beautiful sunset. I have marveled at the way you handle every challenge, how determined you are to get through. My deepest wish is that, someday, you see yourself the way I do.

The realization will always
start from within.

From where your heart and
soul come together
and the symphony begins.

Plant your feet firmly on the
ground; start each step with
a deep breath.

Know that, for every moment
you feel you cannot go on,
the night may be long,
and sometimes it's easier to quit,
but the sunrise will always
and forever be worth it.

How I wish I could bottle
her kindness sometimes.

The way she waters the weeds
in her garden with as much care
as the flowers.

The way she insists on the beauty
of the moon as much as the sun.

She doesn't choose who receives
her kindness, because she gives
her kindness to everyone.

She does not deny a day or night
of her kindness, for every morning
she emerges, with the will to bring
home the light.

It was as though
she had been here before.

She knew of the world's mistakes
and wanted to repair them
with her thoughtfulness.

What else could explain the way
she spoke so softly to those in need,
or so gently to those who had suffered.

It was as though she had come
into the world, and into my life,
just to make it a little brighter.

You will always need someone. Even if it is just one person, in an entire ocean filled with souls, whom you can call at three in the morning and talk about your day. Someone who is always in the room cheering the loudest. Someone who hands you the ice cream tub because they know you'll want to finish it. Someone who is excited to hear about all your dreams and plans, who is there when some of those dreams and plans fall through. Someone who will hold your hand through every win and every loss. Someone who will fight for you without question and love you without expectation. Someone who will always want to see you rise once more.

The world doesn't teach you that you can break up with a friend too. And it will hurt. You will grieve a broken heart in the same way you will feel like you are drowning in all the waves of missing them. You will still want to call them; ask them about their day; share something that made you smile; or hang out in the driveway, staring at the stars for a while. This person, who knew you inside and out, suddenly isn't in your life anymore. Your soul aches for them, in the way you are still hoping they'll walk back through the door. You look for them in every moment of the day, wishing they would appear, that they'll emerge like the sun, and the skies won't be so gray.

Let me tell you a story about a girl I met one spring, when I didn't think very much of anything. We met in a bar when her friend tapped me on the shoulder, told me her friend was a little shy, but when I looked over at her for the first time, I couldn't imagine why. She asked if she could buy me a drink, but I told her I would buy her one instead, and then we talked for hours, about how she loved the smell of cinnamon, eating cereal for dinner, and that her favorite color was red. She told me she loved Sunday markets and that her apartment was covered in plants; she told me her parents didn't always understand her and that she never missed a chance to dance. So, we went out for a while, and even if we didn't have all that much in common, I thought about her nearly every day, and it was enough to make me smile. Six months later, for my birthday, she gave me a journal, inscribed, "You can be anything, if you believe." And now, years later, even if we don't talk anymore, I just wanted to thank her for pushing me to achieve.

You will have people walk
into your life, and you will love them,
but they will never quite understand
what makes you, well, you.

Then you will have people walk
into your life and, even in the silence,
they will always know what you need.

These are not just people;
these are the pieces of your soul,
returning to you.

I've been thinking about the way people say, "Of course I'll help," or, "Do you need me to carry that for you?" I've been thinking about the way people hold open a door as you run to make it through, and they reply with a smile when you say, "Thank you." I've been thinking about the way people band together in times of trouble, like notes and melodies to create a song and, within the song, you find people's compassion and willingness to help, even if it's all night long. I've been thinking about the way people stop to help someone else cross the road, or rescue an animal far from home, or remind a stranger they're not alone. I've been thinking about the way someone starts laughing and it's impossible not to laugh along. I've been thinking there are more people willing to rise to a cause than there are who will retreat, more people willing to say, "We are all here, and we belong."

It has always been the way people speak of the things they love that in turn gives me a will to rise each day. The dreams people have or the hopes they hold on to stirs something deep within my soul. That is the way I like to see people the most. So, I want to know what colors you dream in, if you've ever tasted double chocolate fudge, what your favorite memory is, what is the most recent place you cried. If you prefer milk chocolate or dark chocolate or no chocolate at all, how many times you've spoken hopes into a new sunrise, and whose name you think of every time you close your eyes. For any time we are not together and life keeps us apart, I'll think of you in those moments, because people are the most beautiful when they speak of the things they hold in their heart.

Five years ago, I lived across the road from a widow. Every day, I would see her emerge on the porch and give the mailman a wave. When it was raining, she would greet him by the driveway, hold the umbrella over his head as he walked the path to her front door and handed her the mail. And it warmed me, to see how happy she was every time another letter arrived, but I couldn't quite understand why. Until, one day, collecting my own mail, I asked her, and she told me her husband had written a thousand notes of gratitude, to be delivered to her each day. Because a day that starts with gratitude always shines a little brighter that way.

I have made a home from my heart. I have hung daisies in the window and painted the walls yellow. I have tended to the dust and let light spill into all the corners and cracks. I have learned that the end of each year won't be the same as the last. I have learned that I won't have control over every little detail or the moments that come knocking at my door. I have learned that some people will always give and others will take and take, and take a little more. I have learned that, despite the wind, or rain, or sunshine, I can control the way someone feels every time they walk into my home. And my hope is, if they choose to stay or to leave, at the very least, my home will remind them they'll never walk alone.

I will look for you,
in every brushstroke
of my favorite painting.

I will listen for you,
in the beat of my heart
and rhythm of my soul.

I will reach for you,
in the dark of the night,
searching for all your light.

I will dream of you,
in every skyline
and every act of strength.

And you will emerge,
so wonderful in your joy,
so beautiful in your existence.

It is the same story
written one thousand times;
there is you and a lonely night,
and you feel alone.

You feel hurt and broken, and you
wonder why your best is never enough.

But, the truth is, you will read this story
to yourself many times over.

And if you accept the hurt and the
loneliness as nothing more than friends
who need a place to stay,
then you will make room for them,
acknowledge them, and also remind them
that everything is going to be okay.

Against the backdrop of a blue sky
and a tree-lined garden,
she made a promise to herself
to start each day with gratitude
in her heart and kindness in her hands.

She made a promise to breathe the air deep
into her lungs and treat each living thing
with grace and humility.

She made a promise to the sky, the wind,
and the earth that she would appreciate
the little things and value every person's worth.

My hope
is that, instead
of reminding someone
of their weakness
and kicking them
when they feel down,
we learn to give them
part of our own strength,
hold out our hand,
tell them everything
will be better once more,
so long as we lean
on our friends.

I look for love, the way it emerges from the soul, how different it looks on every person, from the young to the between to the old. How a simple smile could make someone's whole day. How a hello to your neighbor might be the only hello they've had all week. How we really do have time to stop and let people cross the street. How people's warmth really radiates, and it is enough light to challenge the sun. How much value there is in spreading kindness and love.

Time Will Tell

So, you said one day, I am to try a new thing
and you may think it's a little strange
Into our lives, this new path I will bring
but my life and dreams have decided to change

You said, all that I am inside longs to be
part of something more
There is another way my destiny must go
another dream to be fulfilled more
important than before

So, off down the new path you went
one foot in front of the other
and for all the time you have spent
I couldn't be any prouder

The dreams that live inside your soul
were forged billions of years ago
so to follow them is to become whole
the most beautiful thing you'll ever know

So, if you ever feel small or perhaps a little unworthy
know that your dreams are the biggest part of you
If you ever feel uncertain or perhaps a little lonely
know that you are capable in everything you do

And if you ever feel like closing all the doors
on the days doubts flare and so too fear
just remember from my heart to yours
you are here because you belong here.

That is what frightens them—
the power inside women.

For if we rise, they will fall.

Everything is always to contain us,
to overwrite our stories,
to belittle us and control our bodies.

But I believe in a woman's resolve,
her mind, and her grace.

How she can take back her story
and allow her magic to fill every space.

I liked to line my windowsill with empty honey and jelly jars—the rain would roll in from the hills, and I would watch the jars fill with water. One year, I met the love of my life, and she would watch the jars fill with rain too. She would say, "Some of the jars are not catching the rain; let me move them." And I replied, "I love you, but I need to move the jars myself." The jars were like the empty holes in my heart, made by all the people who had come before, who had refused to watch the rain. But these holes were never made to be filled by someone else; they were created to teach me that I can mend my own wounds.

I don't focus
on how many times
I have needed to heal
inside the cocoon
but rather all the times
I have grown
my wings again—
and emerged the next day.

You have to sit with it until it passes. And it will pass. I am not saying that the feelings will leave and never return. Hell, last week, I thought the world was ending. But that's just the way it happens; you truly believe life is over, and then the next day you wake up and you realize it's not. But you still have to sit with those feelings—the pain, the anguish, the worry, and the regret. You let them out into the open, unearth them from the rubble that has collapsed on top of your heart, and you breath in the new air. Through every new breath comes a new moment, and in every new moment is a chance to let the hurt pass.

Metamorphosis itself isn't happiness—
the process can be long, and haunting.
But it is the result that *brings* happiness.
The way you rise to the surface again,
and you realize the journey was worth it.

We went through a time when we were not on the same page. You had your dreams, and I had mine, and we were caught in the middle somewhere, like two hearts on each end of a seesaw, trying to keep it stable. We had asked each other if we thought it was the end. What would we do if we couldn't find our way back? But, during this time, we learned something beautiful—that it was never about finding our way back or holding on to our past selves; instead, it was about the way we moved forward and embraced our transformations. And when we realized this, the memory came flooding back, the reasons we had fallen in love. It had never gone anywhere; it had always been with us. The truth was that we only have one life, and I wanted to spend mine with you. The love I have for you, it runs so deep, through valleys and over mountain peaks, through bright stars and city streets— and I remembered it. There I was, and I could hear your heartbeat in every song, see your smile in every morning, feel your touch in every breath of air. The uncertainty faded away, the pages lined up, and then gratitude set in, to know that the love of my life could also be my best friend; we understood, just because life around us changes doesn't mean it's the end.

There is no magic answer, no silver platter, no map that points to where the healing is hidden. The healing is felt—it emerges through hope—and you reach a place of realization: that it's about renewal, rewriting, and your persistence to redefine. You redefine what it means to transform every time you get knocked off your feet. You rewrite the story every time someone tries to erase your voice, and your hope is renewed every time you climb back out of the cave.

We are told to be afraid. That if we command and live our truth, then the world will no longer accept us. I can't always explain it—this feeling that exists in the very core of who I know myself to be—but it holds itself in a way that cannot be broken. It walks through the world and says, *This is me; I am who I am, and I am not going to bend my truth for anyone.* I do this because it took me such a long time to arrive here; to accept the way that I am; to honor the way my heart chose to love; to acknowledge that I am not different, I simply exist. And I choose to hold on to this courage and not to apologize for the way I am, because the day I finally permitted myself to open the door, I was flooded in light. I carry this light, and it will never allow such darkness in the world to rule my heart.

There is something about dragonflies, my mother would always say, so beautiful in the way they fly, so graceful to watch. One spring, I noticed little nymphs on the stems of lily pads, down in the creek at the end of my garden, and so I stayed for a while, to watch. Sure enough, the nymphs climbed out of the water, emerging from their shells and stretching their wings to fly away. And I understood that this is what it means to watch reinvention, to see someone find their worth. So beautiful in the way they learn to fly, such grace in the way they have healed.

It is simple to say that you could never force something to come true—but how many of us try anyway? We try to make love work, even if it's not meant for us. We try to make someone stay, even if it's better to let them go. We try to convince our hearts of things, even though our minds already know. We try to talk ourselves into going down a road, even though we know it will lead nowhere. And perhaps it's one of the greatest lessons to learn—the forest will grow where it is planted, the sky will light up when the sun and moon are called, the ocean will come and go with the tides. There are many things you cannot control, especially the way life flows and collides.

There are billions of souls on this earth,
all with many hopes and lots of dreams.
Some days struggling to see their worth,
through life's up and downs and in-betweens.

While it seems easy to look the other way,
perhaps you could instead spare a little time
to breathe through the worries of the day
and choose to say something kind.

Like—just look how far you have come
on your journey through this change.
Look at all the good you have done
and strength pumping through your veins.

For, underneath, there is a story to be told,
with a beautiful heart, always ready to sing.
For the surest way to break free of the fold
is to remind someone of the joy they bring.

The Rebirth

I don't know if you need to hear this,
but keep going.
Even though, lately, the days feel
overwhelming.
Even if the notes in your journal
have not made any sense in a while.
It's still your story—
and your story is breathtaking.
People will try to take it from you,
rob you of the forgiveness
that blooms inside your chest.
And we are so hell-bent on loving
people who never notice us
in a crowded room.
But you deserve to be noticed.
I know,
because I see you, I hear you, I love you.
In time, I hope you will see
that you have the capacity to unearth
a new you—
and you will dust off the dirt,
and you will survive.

So, here it is—more words to encourage us to try again. And they can seem a little mundane, dull, against the rage inside a heart, timid in the face of a soul so desperate to feel again. Change is hard. Peeling back skin to reinvent yourself feels like a mountain too steep to climb. But I like to think of life in the same way I think of flowing water. Sometimes, the creeks, the streams, the lakes will all be dry. Filled with carnage, broken branches, dead leaves, dust, and dirt. But then the rain comes, and all the tiny droplets of water merge together to create the river once more. You need words of encouragement, no matter how many times you reread them, for they can make you stronger than you were before.

I started to truly live on the day I decided no one else was going to control my narrative. I decided that I was not meek, or worthless, or unable to stand on my own two feet. And I promised myself, day by day, week by week, that I would not be spoken down to or treated less than I deserved. The shift started with the rise of the sun, the turn of the tide, the whisper of the trees. For to command respect is to say— even to the people we love—I am here, and I am powerful.

It has been a beautiful thing to watch you grow. To see your power rise from within. The surety you have within yourself—you do not need to tear others down to know your own worth. I suppose you have always walked with grace, but every step is different now, more assured. It is one of my favorite things about you, that your ability to move through the world comes from a security deep within your heart. There is no need to step on others to arrive at the place you are headed, no need to cast words of shame, no desire to take when all that you have become has been based on your own reflection.

We will leave the world someday.

You will leave; I will leave;
we will all leave
and go back to the stars.

And the world will continue on
without us.

And it won't matter how we arrived
or how we went—
but rather how we lived
when we were here.

And I do hope you live—
with a sense of purpose in your step,
with an open heart for your friends,
with gratitude in every morning.

In the quiet of the night, the universe will whisper many words—*why you are here, what your purpose is, who you are when the world sleeps*—and it may always seem as though you don't belong anywhere, like your soul was not meant for the body you are in. But you must remember this: you cannot begin to understand yourself if you spend your whole life avoiding the things you feel. You cannot find your place if you outrun difficult conversations. You cannot reply to the stars if you refuse your own light. So, you must use every feeling and join them all together to create the tapestry of your existence, for, in this universe, you are the thread, the stitch, and the sewer.

For as long as you live, there will always be something waiting—in the shadows and in the light—and the truth is not to be afraid. For there will be days that hit you like a ton of bricks and others that present you with a bouquet of sunflowers; somewhere in between the good and the bad, you'll learn to continue living.

Grief can be many things—an ache for those we have lost, dismay for the dreams that have sailed on by, regret for the moments we allowed to slip between our fingers. Sometimes it feels endless, like walking through an open field, expecting to see all the miles around you, but the night is dark, and the fireflies stay hidden. You will throw your arms in front of you, behind you, all around you, desperate to grab hold of anything that will remind you, you are still part of the world, still anchored to a life worth living. And when hope finds you broken on the floor, it will wrap its arms around you and tell you to let go—for grief can root us in place, but starting again is trusting the wings of hope to fly once more.

Perhaps the reason
so many choose to hide
behind closed doors
is for the fear there will
be no one to greet them
on the other side.

It is a simple, beautiful thing
about humans—
we want to mean something,
to someone.

We want to know our worth
and our existence matter.

So, if you ever have the chance
to remind someone of their
importance, and of their worth,
that just by being here,
the world is a little better—
open the door.

It was always fear and self-doubt that stopped me from climbing the mountain, boarding the train, leaving the cave, or breaking free of the cocoon. There were so many things I could have done, so many moments that have now passed and will never return. There was a deep sadness in this realization but also something I did not expect. I was forced to ask myself, *What would I do if fear did not hold me back? Who would I be in this world, where would I go, and what could I become?* And, now, I understand—you look Fear dead in the eyes, and you say, "You can be here, but you will not stand in my way."

May you always have hope for tomorrow
and find joy in every sunset and sunrise.
May you marvel in all the ways you grow
and find home in each other's bright eyes.

May you spend each day side by side
as lovers, partners, and best friends.
May you laugh through every turning tide,
through all of life's turns and bends.

And if you ever lose your way,
just know you can step in time together—
because nothing brightens a day
like two hearts beating in sync forever.

The scariest thing about starting again is learning a new language. There you were in life; you knew every syllable, word, character, and sentence. You knew how to speak, and then suddenly everything went quiet. The worst day of your life was realizing you would never speak the same language again, for it had been and it had gone. But that is the most beautiful thing about language; we are always finding new ways to use our voice.

Time Will Tell

It was always a risk to love you—
I knew what they would say and
all the ways they would try to keep us apart
But the way my hand fits with yours
and that feeling in my chest

    always you

You kissed me once for every letter
in my name, told me that in the moments
that felt too complicated and out of reach

you would breathe, and I'd be right there
on your lips

    forever

I heard once of a theory that
we are all from the same soul.

You've been every person
that's ever lived,
and they've been you.

And so, if this is true—
and that the most important thing
is to tell the people we love
how we cherish them, love them,
and are proud of them—

then it is also true to believe
these things of ourselves.

This is the thing they don't tell you about time—you turn thirty, and you still feel like you're fifteen. More than a decade has past, but you still like chocolate chips hidden in ice cream, good-morning texts from your mom, and movies that make you dream. Some days, you can't even take a step forward without needing the hand of someone to hold, or words to remind you that you're doing just fine, or a long hug to make you feel safe. When you're young, you want to believe everyone much older than you knows the secret to life, but then suddenly you arrive, and you realize you don't. The years go on, and you are still young at heart, only with more responsibilities and the assumption we are always in control. It is a funny dance, between the young and old, but perhaps we can learn from each other that life can be messy but also takes us by surprise, through every twist and every fold.

I have written a thousand poems, filled with many things. Some I looked back on and I don't remember them to be mine. But perhaps this is the beauty of it all, that words reinvent themselves over time. They can mean one thing one season and something else another. I could read them years from the moment they were written, and they will hold an entirely different meaning. This is what gives me hope; we can be born again and again.

One morning, I was in a hurry. I had made my coffee, left the mug on the counter, and turned around to pop the bread in the toaster. As I turned, I knocked the mug over, spilling coffee onto the floor—and then you walked in and asked why I was so upset, and I pointed to the mess. And you looked at the mess and then at me with a smile. "Only a few drops my love," you said. "Your mug is still half full."

Things will always happen—toast burns, coffee spills, life wreaks a little havoc. But we often assume the puddle is bigger than it is. We will convince ourselves the whole mug is now empty, when, really, it's still half full.

My grandmother said to me once, over shortbread biscuits and tea, that in her life she has learned many lessons, and she hopes she has passed them on to me. She said beauty is measured in the respect and honesty someone shows you and that one of the greatest wonders of the world is that the sky can be many shades of blue. She said you will try and fail many times before you succeed, that you will feel lost from time to time, but it will never invalidate your dreams. She said people's opinions of you and the love you choose in your life will never dictate your worth, that there is importance in family and grounded friendships, there is healing in a deep belly laugh and value in a good book and a bubble bath. She said that being different is not an anomaly, that sincerity comes from taking responsibility and heartfelt apologies. She said beautiful memories are made from living in the moment and, most importantly, reinventing oneself is always timeless.

It is a heavy thought to have
that while I dance and laugh,
another in the world suffers
alone inside their head.

Where was I on the night
someone else wanted to end it all?

And so, I remind myself, as often
as I can—underneath the skin,
and bones, and shell of a person
is the story of a soul that needs
a gentle word and a kind smile
to pull back the curtain.

Here are some things I thought you should know: You make a difference just by existing. You inspire me to continue forward, knowing that hope can be found in running rivers, or whispering trees, or a small sprout after a flower withers. I hear your voice, as clearly as I hear the waves as they crash onto the shore. How your ideas deserve to be listened to, acknowledged, and adored. You light up every room you walk into; it doesn't matter if you are having a good day or a bad day, you are still worthy of victory. It may feel you have begun again too many times, but how wonderful it is to live many, many lives.

ALWAYS

They say it's just a poem, that it doesn't mean a thing,
but how can it be just a poem, with all the heart it brings.
They say it's just some words written on a page with a pen,
but isn't it beautiful, the way it can feel a little like a friend?

If on the nights you are tired and alone in the dark,
then perhaps the words you read give you a little spark.
If on the days you feel lost in all that you've ever known,
then perhaps every rhyme can build you a bright new home.

And, in the end, the words may say, "This is how life
feels to me;
do you feel the same? Maybe together we can try to
break free."
So, to them, I say, "A poem can always be so much more—
a gentle reminder to be better than perhaps we were before."

You cannot hope to evolve,
if you blame everyone else
around you.

When you try to find the answers
in the actions of others
and not those of yourself.

It is difficult to take a step back
and look at the picture you have painted.
But the picture can never change
if you are not willing to try new strokes.

When was the last time you stopped to congratulate yourself—for all that you have done and all the ways you have strived to keep moving? When was the last time you said to yourself, *I will never be who I was before, and I am proud of this.* When was the last time you stood in front of the mirror and recognized all the resilience looking back at you? Regret meets us in a darkened hallway and tries to convince us the lights will never turn back on. But, despite this, you have spent each day searching for the road to redemption. When you turn on the light, don't forget it was your hands that ignited the spark.

Life doesn't stop,
even in the midst
of your healing—
you will still laugh,
still find joy,
still experience love.

Sometimes, the ability
to carry on is
strengthened
by all the times
you continue to
live in the moment.

Time Will Tell

There's that feeling,
always coming back around,
to make you feel alone,
like you don't belong anywhere
and haven't found your home.

But remember this—
on a calm day, the wind settles
between blades of grass and the
sweetness of low-hanging honeysuckle.

Even if you cannot see beyond
the next minute or the next hour,
your patience can be found between
fields of color—
your ability to begin again
can be seen through all the miles
you've already traveled.

You shatter, and the pieces scatter out all around you—and it is easy to demand others to search for them, to gather every piece and hand them back to you. But, as it happens, what describes growth the most is when you are frustrated, or sad, or angry, you choose not to take it out on those around you. When you stop in time to reflect on the feelings you have, to acknowledge they are valid and important because they are felt by you and they are your own feelings, you are the only one who can climb the ladder. Oh, but once you reach the top, you can see the whole picture sprawled out before you, and you'll understand, you'll always be a puzzle, trying to arrange every piece.

As dark as the past may be,
Forgiveness lives here too—
it whispers to you, "Carry on
upward, toward the sun."

I cared too much;
that was the problem.
I was a colosseum and
allowed everyone inside,
to take shelter—until
the cracks started to form
and eventually I came
crashing down.

Now, the skies are clearer,
and I have rebuilt,
but I am stronger now,
and I still care—
but not at the expense
of my own ability to stand.

I wish I could walk beside you,
remind you of the beauty
in every step.

I wish I could sit beside you,
remind you of all the moments
you are your own maker of hope.

I wish I could greet you
at the end of the road,
remind you of all the ways you are
your own creator of restoration.

I wish for you to truly believe one day
you are more than "sometimes"—
you are
"always."

Even in the dark, you must remember that your future is still bright. That sometimes you will burn through the atmosphere and pieces of you will end up scattered in thousands of different places. But every journey you take to seek them out will shape you into the brightest star you are yet to become. Don't lose sight of the bigger picture. Don't be a singular star, when you were born to be the whole galaxy.

You had asked me
where I'd come from
and where I thought
I might be headed.

So, I'd thought about
all the long and forgotten
pathways I'd walked, all
the mountains I'd climbed
with an ache in my chest,
the woods I had traveled,
toward the eventual healing.

And I'd looked back at you,
with steady eyes, and I replied,

"I've been on my way to you."

Your whole life won't be solved in a single day—
and I hope you find the courage to understand
that it is acceptable to slow down, to take your time,
to just be in every moment.

To exist is to live and to also break.

Healing is much like a pile of leaves. The pile does not
appear in an instant. It takes many falling leaves,
slowly, one by one, adding to the pile.

Time Will Tell

We've reached another ending to the tale
and another silver lining to the storm—
for, no matter how many times we fail,
we can always find renewal and reform.

And while it seems time will always tell—
perhaps the truth emerges from your soul,
for, in the moments you stumbled and fell,
you learned many lessons to make you whole.

You grew within the warmest cocoon
and dreamed and hoped and changed.
You ran your own race, to your own tune,
despite all the burdens and all the pain.

And in the times you are afraid to awaken,
just remember in your heart what is true—
for all the long days and steps you have taken,
the person who takes flight is always you.

An Ode to the Butterfly Story*

*Someone once told me the story of a man and a butterfly,
a story that I'd like to share with you.*

 nce, in the deepest part of a beautiful garden, a man found a cocoon, small, silky, barely hanging on to the branches of the tree. Over time, the man noticed a small opening. So, he sat down by the cocoon and watched for a long while, expecting to see a butterfly emerge.

Eventually, he began to notice the butterfly, as she slowly pushed her body through the opening. But, soon, the man realized the opening was not large enough. The butterfly was not going to be able to squeeze its body through.

The man, unwilling to let the butterfly die, decided to offer help. Carefully, he began to make the opening larger. Prying it open so that the butterfly could finally emerge.

And the butterfly did emerge, but her wings were damaged, and her body too. The man wondered if perhaps she just needed time to grow her wings and repair her body, and she would take flight.

---

*Adapted from a blog by Paul Coelho from a story sent in by Sonaira D'Avila.

But he had misunderstood, and the butterfly's wings remained damaged, and her body stayed shriveled, and so she carried on in her life, never able to fly.

For while the man's intentions were kind, by not allowing the butterfly to go through the struggle of her restricted cocoon, her wings did not strengthen as they were supposed to, and her body did not grow in the way it should have.

In life, it is the struggle that strengthens our resolve. Without the struggle, we will never understand what it means to fly.

Thank you for reading this book.

I hope you enjoyed reading it as much as I enjoyed writing it. You can stay up-to-date with all my latest news and projects via my website, www.peppernell.com.

Feel free to write to me via courtney@pepperbooks.org.

Pillow Thoughts app now available on iOS and Android stores, worldwide and on all devices— download yours today for your daily poetry!

Andrews McMeel Publishing
a division of Andrews McMeel Universal
1130 Walnut Street, Kansas City, Missouri 64106

www.andrewsmcmeel.com

23 24 25 26 27 MCN 10 9 8 7 6 5 4 3 2 1

ISBN: 978-1-5248-7212-0

Library of Congress Control Number: 2022949709

Illustrations by Justin Estcourt

Editor: Patty Rice
Art Director: Diane Marsh
Production Editor: Elizabeth A. Garcia
Production Manager: Shona Burns

ATTENTION: SCHOOLS AND BUSINESSES
Andrews McMeel books are available at quantity discounts with
bulk purchase for educational, business, or sales promotional
use. For information, please e-mail the Andrews McMeel
Publishing Special Sales Department: sales@amuniversal.com.